Rules for Young Friends

A Training Manual for Children

by
Gregg & Josh
Harris

To our friends.

Noble Publishing Associates
P.O. Box 2250, Gresham, Oregon 97030

Special arrangements may be made to use these
materials and host these
presentations for fund raising and
educational purposes.

For details contact:
Director of Special Events
Noble Publishing Associates
P.O. Box 2250,
Gresham, Oregon 97080

Printed in the United States of America

ISBN 0-923463-64-X

Table of Contents

How to Use This Training Manual for Children

Dear Parent of a Young Friend,

Friends!?! Many of your child's best and worst experiences in life will involve his friends. No one can encourage him better, or hurt him worse, than his first friends. His attitudes toward himself and others are planted in the playtimes, watered with the tears and battered by the storms of his young friendships. His honesty, integrity, character and other things he may not understand, will none the less affected by the friends of his childhood.

In many ways a child is like an immigrant, first in his own home and later in his neighborhood. An immigrant is someone who has just arrived in a new country. Because he is new, he is naturally confused about what he may and may not do in his new surroundings. Unwritten rules seem to define what is acceptable and unacceptable behavior . Trial and error is required to discover the boundaries. And the moods of local authorities seem to change the rules from day to day. A person in this situation needs a trusted authority to teach him the rules so that he can stay out of trouble and get on with the adventure of life.

In the same way, your child arrives fresh from hispreschool years with a burst of enthusiasm. His church and neighborhood are full of other children. He wants to play with them, and they want to play with him. Unfortunately, in many he is unprepared for what awaits him. Even if he has been prepared by good parents, his first playmates are likely to be unprepared to be kind, sharing, well behaved friends. Regardless of who is the leader and who is the follower, these young friends will be getting into trouble for breaking rules they don't even know exist. Like the newly arrived immigrant, they need an orientation to the rules for having and being a good friend.

Many Christian parents now use *The 21 Rules of This House Training Kit* developed by Gregg & Sono Harris as the basis of social order in their homes. If you do not already have that basic kit, I suggest that you order it. The laminated master list of *The 21 Rules* is designed to be posted with magnets on your refrigerator door. Those easy-to-understand house rules define the behavioral boundaries for everyone in your home, and thereby eliminate a major source of frustration for you and your child. Even though *The Rules for Young Friends* build on the foundation laid by the 21 House Rules the two sets of rules can be used separately.

But *having* rules is one thing, *teaching* them to a child is another. That is why this "training manual" for children has been included in your training kit. This volume offers a series of eleven simple illustrations by our household graphic artist Josh Harris (age 14) to help your younger child understand and remember the **Rules for Young Friends**.

To begin, I suggest that you and your child read the Training Manual straight through like a book several times. Then read through it more slowly each day, stopping at various illustrations to talk about specific rules you would like him to pay special attention to. Guide him in thinking of other examples of a child like himself keeping or breaking the particular rule he needs to learn. If your child enjoys coloring, allow him to color each illustration as he studies it. You may wish to photo-copy each page so that several children can color the same illustration at the same time.

Additional instructions and suggestions for using *Rules for Young Friends* are included in this **Training Kit for Young Friends**. You might also benefit from listening to (or viewing) "Training Grounds in Child Discipline," by this author. In the tape set, available in both audio and video formats, I present the biblical concept of "training grounds" for teaching children to be faithful and obedient in small areas of responsibility. Training Grounds, in combination with the *21 Rules*, give children the structure and the flexibility they need to become more responsible for their actions. *Rules for Young Friends* follows the same principles. Greater liberty should be granted only to those who are being faithful with the liberty they already have.

All of these child training materials are developed and written by the Harris Family and published by *Noble Publishing Associates*. We invite you to use our Mail Order Form in the appendix to order other items from Noble. **The 21 Rules Training Kit**, and this **Training Kit for Young Friends** make excellent gifts for friends and family with younger children. Grandparents enjoy using these materials to support you in the training of their grandchildren. Sunday School teachers also use them to help keep order in class.

Thank you for allowing our family to serve your family. May God richly bless you as you train up your children in the way that they should go.

For Christ and the Christian Family,

Gregg Harris for the Harris Family
Gregg, Sono, Josh, Joel, Alex & Brett
May 1, 1989

Proverbs for Friends

Proverbs13:20   He who walks with the wise grows wise, but a companion of fools suffers harm.

Proverbs 12:22   The Lord detests lying lips, but he delights in men who are truthful.

Proverbs 17:14   Starting a quarrel is like breaching a dam; so drop the matter before a dispute breaks out.

Proverbs 26:18-19 Like a madman shooting firebrands or deadly arrows is a man who deceives his neighbor and says, "I was only joking!"

Proverbs 15:1   A gentle answer turns away wrath, but a harsh word stirs up anger.

Proverbs 18:13   He who answers before listening-- that is his folly and his shame.

Proverbs 11:27   He who seeks good finds goodwill, but evil comes to him who searches for it.

Proverbs 19:4   Wealth brings many friends, but a poor man's friend deserts him.

Proverbs 19:17   He who is kind to the poor lends to the Lord, and he will reward him for what he has done.

Proverbs 25:28   Like a city whose walls are broken down is a man who lacks self-control.

Proverbs 13:1   A wise son heeds his father's instruction, but a mocker does not listen to rebuke.

Kids' Stuff

Dear Parents,

Here we are again! This is my second shot at illustrating and I'm enjoying it even more. With my first book, *The 21 Rules of this House*, I was a little nervous. But its great reception and the hundreds of letters we've received from families telling us how much it has blessed them have given my confidence a boost.

Our family has been using *Rules for Young Friends* for quite some time and we have seen its benefits with my younger brother, Joel. That's why we have decided to offer it to others. We believe it will greatly benefit your Christian family.

Although having friends at a young age is wonderful, without proper guidelines it can cause children to develop bad attitudes towards work and the rest of their family. I hope these rules will help build your family as much as they have ours.

In Christ,

Josh Harris
(age 14)

1.

Parents decide when, where & with whom their children may play.

2.

Friends
may not go inside
anyone's home,
or go anywhere else,
until everyone's parents
have given their permission
to do so.

3.

Friends
must respect one another's house rules & standards at all times & in all places.

4.

Friends
must be friendly
toward every member
of one another's
family.

5.

Friends
may play
with one another's toys
if they are willing
to ask first,
be careful,
& help put things away
before leaving.

6.

Friends
may give or loan things
to one another
only if they have first
received permission
to do so
from one another's parents.

7.

Friends
may not distract
one another
from cheerfully completing
family chores
& school assignments.

8.

Friends
must not cause
one another
to miss
church services
or other important
family activities.

9.

Family members
are our most
important friends.
Therefore,
brothers & sisters
must be loyal
to one another.

10.

Children
who do or say
things to cause
one another to be
disobedient
will not be allowed
to play together again
unless they apologize
to one another's
parents.

11.

Friends
may be included
in one another's
special family activities
if they have shown
that they can play together
well on other
occasions.

_____

_____

_____

_____

_____

_____

_____

_____

_____

_____

Write your own rule.

Draw your own illustration.

Kids' Stuff
Mail Order Form—Photocopy Master

The Home Taught Pen Pal Service

Welcome to the largest home school pen pal service in the world! Over 2000 kids have been matched up since 1984. Kids all across the U.S. now enjoy writing to one another, sharing their interests and their experiences as Christian home school students. There's no better way to get your children to practice their hand writing or typing skills than to have them write regularly to a pen pal. Many pen pals arrange to meet one another while on vacations. They read books together, trade school project ideas and send Christmas cards and gifts to one another. In other words, home taught pen pals enjoy a lasting friendship.

If you would like one or more pen pals for your home schooling children, just PRINT in the blanks below, the name, age and gender of each child. Then send this form to me with $3 per pen pal. Don't forget to fill in the mailing address information at the bottom of this form. I'll match your child up with home schoolers somewhere in the United States. **It sometimes takes me 2 to 3 months to match up the right ages and genders** so please be sure to have each child write to his new pen pal(s) as soon as he receives one.

Child's Name _____ Age_____ Gender M F $3.00

Child's Name _____ Age_____ Gender M F $3.00

Child's Name _____ Age_____ Gender M F $3.00

"Just Enough" Stationery

When do you need stationery? How about when you have to write an official letter to a school official or make an order to a curriculum supplier? Or when you need to write business letters for your family business? Or when you have an important Press Release to mail out concerning a home school support group activity? Or even when you just want to write a nice personal letter to a friend or family member? These are times when you'll be glad you have "Just Enough" Stationery from Kid's Stuff.

Now for less than you could have the typesetting done locally, you can have twenty copies of your own beautifully typeset stationery for your home school, your family business, your home school support group and your personal correpondence. Choose from three classic type face styles. You'll receive "just enough" stationery to meet all your needs at the lowest possible cost. And, at no extra charge, I'll include a Master Copy of each stationery letterhead you order. That way you can have additional stationery printed locally as you need it.

To order, just fill out the information below. Be sure to PRINT carefully. Use the reverse side if you have different addresses for each set of stationery. Select Type Face 1, 2 or 3 below for each letterhead you order. Allow 4 to 6 weeks for delivery.

#1. **Gresham Christian Academy**

#2. *The Smith Family Business*

#3. **John S. Doe**

Order 2 or more for only $7 each

Type Face #

Home School Name _____ $7.95 @

Business Name _____ $7.95 @

Personal Name _____ $7.95 @

Mailing Name _____

Address _____

City _____ State_____ Zip _____

Phone (_____) _____

Check #

_____

Totals

Total $

Mail with check payable to: Kid's Stuff to 6920 S.E. Hogan Road, Gresham, OR 97080

1.

Parents decide
when, where & with whom
their children may play.

2.

Friends

may not go inside anyone's home,

or go anywhere else,

until everyone's parents have

given their permission to do so.

3.

Friends

must respect one another's

house rules & standards

at all times & in all places.

4.

Friends
must be friendly
toward every member
of one another's family.

5.

Friends

may play with one another's toys
if they are willing to ask first,
be careful, & help put things away
before leaving.

6.

Friends

may give or loan things

to one another only if they have first

received permission to do so

from one another's parents.

7.

Friends

may not distract one another

from cheerfully completing

family chores & school assignments.

8.

Friends

must not cause one another

to miss church services

or other important family activities.

9.

Family members
are our most important friends.
Therefore, brothers & sisters
must be loyal to one another.

10.

Children who do or say things
to cause one another to be disobedient
will not be allowed to play together
again unless they apologize
to one another's parents.

11.

Friends

may be included in one another's special family activities if they have shown that they can play together well on other occasions.

Rules for Young Friends

Write your own rule.

Rules for Young Friends

Write your own rule.

Proverbs 11:27

He who seeks good
finds goodwill,
but evil comes to him
who searches for it.

Proverbs 12:22

The Lord detests lying lips,
but he delights in men
who are truthful.

Proverbs 13:1

A wise son heeds
his father's instruction,
but a mocker does not listen
to rebuke.

Proverbs13:20

He who walks with the wise
grows wise,
but a companion of fools
suffers harm.

Proverbs for Young Friends

Proverbs 15:1

A gentle answer turns away wrath,
but a harsh word stirs up anger.

Proverbs 17:14

Starting a quarrel is like
breaching a dam;
so drop the matter
before a dispute breaks out.

Proverbs for Young Friends

Proverbs 18:13

He who answers before listening—
that is his folly and his shame.

Proverbs 19:4

Wealth brings many friends,
but a poor man's friend
deserts him.

Proverbs 19:17

He who is kind to the poor
lends to the Lord,
and he will reward him
for what he has done.

Proverbs 25:28

Like a city whose walls
are broken down
is a man who lacks self-control.

Proverbs 26:18-19

Like a madman shooting firebrands
or deadly arrows
is a man who deceives his neighbor
and says, "I was only joking!"

Rules for Young Friends

1. Parents decide when, where & with whom their children may play.

2. Friends may not go inside anyone's home, or go anywhere else, until everyone's parents have given their permission to do so.

3. Friends must respect one another's house rules & standards at all times and in all places.

4. Friends must be friendly toward every member of one another's family.

5. Friends may play with one another's toys if they are willing to ask first, be careful, & help put things away before leaving.

6. Friends may give or loan things to one another only if they have first received permission to do so from one another's parents.

7. Friends may not distract one another from cheerfully completing family chores & school assignments.

8. Friends must not cause one another to miss church services or other important family activities.

9. Family members are our most important friends. Therefore, brothers & sisters must be loyal to one another.

10. Children who do or say things to cause one another to be disobedient will not be allowed to play together again unless they apologize to one another's parents.

11. Friends may be included in one another's special family activities if they have shown that they can play together well on other occasions.

© Copyright 1989 by Gregg & Josh Harris. Published by Noble Publishing Associates. "Rules for Young Friends" is part of **The Training Kit for Young Friends**, which includes a laminated master copy of the rules, instructions for parents & grandparents, a reproducible coloring book illustrating each rule and eleven individual rule posters. If you do not have the complete kit, you may order one by mailing $11.95 to, Rules for Young Friends, c/o Noble Publishing Associates, P.O. Box 2250, Gresham, OR 97030. Phone 1-800-225-5259

ISBN #0-923463-64-X